Duet for Cannibals

Duet
for Cannibals

A SCREENPLAY BY
Susan Sontag

FARRAR, STRAUS AND GIROUX
NEW YORK

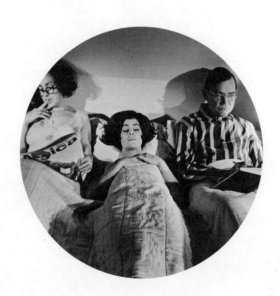

For Susan Taubes (*1928–1969*)

NOTE

The first version of the script of *Duet for Cannibals*, which I wrote in Stockholm in August 1968, was an old-fashioned, numbered shot-by-shot *découpage*, each page divided into two columns, with the image on the left and the dialogue plus sound effects on the right. What follows is the second version, written in early September to facilitate work with the actors, in which I eliminated much of the explicit visual material (indications of how the image was to be framed, specifics of camera movement) and added descriptions of the décor, clothes, and of the characters and their moods.

While preparing this second version of the script, I was also choosing the locations and completing the casting. Agneta Ekmanner, who plays Ingrid, had already agreed to take part in the film in May, during my first, brief visit to Stockholm, when I had only a rough idea of the story in my head. I had asked Adriana Asti to be in the film in July, when I was in Rome, and the part of Francesca was written for her. Gösta Ekman, who plays Tomas, and Lars Ekborg, who plays Bauer, were cast in September.

Filming took place on locations in and around Stockholm in October and November, over a period of six weeks. We had thirty-four shooting days. The film was shot in black and white 35 mm. film with one Arriflex camera; all the dialogue and most of the effects were recorded direct with a Nagra. Since *Duet for Cannibals* was, as the expression goes, edited in the camera, the actual editing, done in February and March 1969, went fairly smoothly. The first screening was at the Cannes

Film Festival, under the auspices of the *Quinzaine des Réalisateurs,* in May 1969.

Although fortified with a detailed script when I began shooting, I had expected that many elements would be altered or dropped in the course of the shooting, and many new things invented and improvised by myself, the cameraman, and the actors. To my surprise, very little of this happened. I was not conscious of feeling, as the film's director, any particular loyalty to myself as the author of the script. But as we began working, and especially when I saw that the actors felt the script was sound and their roles performable as I'd conceived them, there seemed no reason not to follow the script closely throughout the shooting. Because this is what did happen, I'm now publishing what I wrote in September, despite some tiny discrepancies between the script and the finished film, rather than a new, third version. The only change I've made now is to omit eleven sequences (the original script consisted of seventy-five sequences) which I dropped in the editing—in most cases, to keep down the film's length; in two cases, because the sequence simply didn't work. I had wanted *Duet for Cannibals* to run no more than 95 minutes; in the final editing I settled for 104 minutes, though I now regret not having been tougher with the film and sticking to my original resolution.

Susan Sontag

New York
November 1969

CREDITS

WRITTEN AND DIRECTED BY: *Susan Sontag*
PRODUCER: *Göran Lindgren*
EXECUTIVE PRODUCER: *Peter Hald*
PHOTOGRAPHY: *Lars Swanberg / Hans Welin*
SOUND: *Ulf Darin / Kjell Nicklasson*
ASSISTANT TO THE DIRECTOR: *Brita Werkmäster*
CONTINUITY: *Kerstin Eriksdotter*
CLOTHING AND PROPERTIES: *Katerina Lindgren*
ELECTRICIAN: *Ulf Björk*
MAKE-UP: *Tina Johansson / Barbro Holmbring*
EDITOR: *C. O. Skeppstedt*
MIXING: *Sven Fahlén*
MUSIC: *Dvořák, Mahler, Wagner*

CAST

FRANCESCA BAUER: *Adriana Asti*
ARTHUR BAUER: *Lars Ekborg*
TOMAS: *Gösta Ekman*
INGRID: *Agneta Ekmanner*
MRS. GRUNDBERG: *Brita Brunius*
LARS: *Stig Engström*
MAN IN CAFETERIA: *Gunnar Lindqvist*

Duet for Cannibals was produced by Sandrew Film & Teater AB (Sweden). It is distributed by Evergreen Films in the United States and Canada and by Contemporary Films in Great Britain.

Duet for Cannibals

Credits, in plain, book-face black type.

Slow, rhythmic, hammering noise over the credits.

1. Ingrid's room. Day

A big, light, studio-like room with three windows, sparsely
furnished: double bed; small table under the large window
stacked with books; table with two wooden kitchen chairs
against one wall under another window; one comfortable,
seedy upholstered chair; homemade bookshelves filled
with books (mostly paperbacks), some records, and a
portable phonograph; a sink and small stove along another
wall; posters and photographs on several walls, including
a poster of Hugo Blanco, and NLF flag, photographs
of the black athletes at the Mexico Olympics giving
the Black Power salute and a fashion model, and the
front pages of newspapers announcing the death of Robert
Kennedy and the invasion of Czechoslovakia. The general
appearance of the room is messy. Clothes slung over
the chairs, unmade bed, dirty dishes piled up in the
sink. The big window at the far end of the room gives
onto the roof. The window starts about four feet off
the floor, so to get out to the roof one must step up
on the low table stacked with books. From the roof—it
is the eighth floor of a modern apartment building--there
is a spectacular view of the city and water.

The film opens with a close-up of a woman's hand. Silence. The camera pulls back a little, showing the hand picking up a hammer.

Medium shot (from behind): INGRID is nailing up a poster of ARTHUR BAUER. Continuation of the sound heard during the credits. INGRID wears slacks and a sweater. More hammering. She steps back to look at the poster.

2. Ingrid's room. Morning

Medium shot of TOMAS: standing before the small mirror left of the sink, shaving. TOMAS is an ex-student, in his late twenties, intense-looking but somewhat inexpressive facially, methodical but graceful in his movements; there is something faintly abrasive in his manner. He wears jeans and is bare-chested.

INGRID

(*Off*) Coffee?

TOMAS nods yes. Cuts himself. Puts a small Band-Aid on his cheek, while we hear INGRID's voice again, still off, this time flat and impersonal as if she were reading what she says. (Such "narrative" passages will be in quotes throughout the script to distinguish them from lines that are said "off.")

INGRID'S VOICE

"Bauer asked Tomas to come at 6 p.m. tomorrow. And afterwards they would make a schedule for the work."

Medium long shot of INGRID, the first time we get any

real sense of the room. INGRID stands by the phonograph. She is also an ex-student, around twenty-six, pretty, thin, slightly nervous in her movements. She has on different pants and sweater from those she wore in the preceding sequence. She puts on a record: the Prize Song from *Die Meistersinger*.

The camera cuts back to TOMAS, who turns his head and grimaces almost imperceptibly.

> TOMAS
>
> Getting me in the mood for Bauer?

INGRID crosses the room (coming into the shot), stands next to TOMAS.

> INGRID
>
> I love you, you know.

TOMAS smiles faintly, rubs his cheek.

> INGRID
>
> You've cut yourself.

> TOMAS
>
> It's nothing.

INGRID turns to the stove and begins making coffee while TOMAS continues shaving, his back to her. They have the air of two people who have lived together for some time, probably several years. From the stove, INGRID glances fondly at TOMAS from time to time. TOMAS finishes shaving, puts on a sweater, looks at his watch.

> TOMAS
>
> I don't have time for coffee after all. I'm supposed to meet some people now.

6

TOMAS kisses INGRID on the cheek.

TOMAS

See you.

He grabs a jacket from the upholstered chair, slings it over his shoulder, goes out the door. Noise of the door shutting cuts off the music.

3. Ingrid's room. Morning, next day

Medium shot of the bed. INGRID is still sleeping. TOMAS, lying next to her on his right side, propped up on his elbow, is looking at her. He touches her face lightly. Then he lies back and stares ahead.

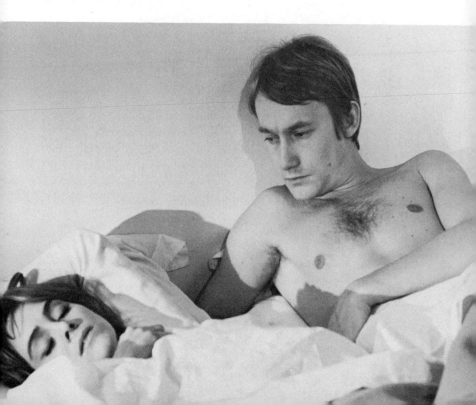

Shot of phonograph on the bookshelf (from TOMAS's point of view). Though the turntable isn't moving, we hear the Prize Song again.

Medium shot of bed. TOMAS, eyes open, is lying on his back. When INGRID stirs, starting to wake up, he pretends to be asleep and pulls the sheet over his head. Music fades. INGRID sits up partially, rubs her eyes, looks over at TOMAS, then reaches to the nighttable to look at her watch. She looks tired and sad. Sound of low-flying airplane.

4. *Entrance to Bauer house. 6 p.m. same day*

The house on the outskirts of Stockholm in which the BAUERS live is a large, well-kept "villa" built in the 1920's or 1930's, surrounded by a large, sloping garden (sundial, lawn furniture, etc.) cut through by steps and a curving flagstone walk. The garage is separate. The front and sides of the property are separated from the street by a five-foot-high stucco wall. The curtains of the windows on the upper floor are always drawn.

The sequence consists of one medium shot. We see TOMAS at the front door, ringing the bell. He seems nervous or shy. After a pause, the BAUERS' housekeeper, MRS. GRUNDBERG, opens the door. She is about fifty-five years old, surly, and limps. TOMAS is as dressed up as he's ever willing to be—a colored shirt, dark pants, jacket, and boots.

TOMAS

How do you do. I have an appointment with Dr. Bauer.

A quizzical look from MRS. GRUNDBERG. Then she stands aside and motions for him to enter.

5. *Library of Bauer house. Minutes later*

A medium-sized room, most of the wall space covered with bookcases containing heavy, scholarly-looking books. A fireplace and a dark brown, L-shaped couch at one end of the room near the door. On the opposite wall, under a window, a beige upholstered couch; in front of the couch, a low table, stacked with magazines; to the left of the couch, a ladder for reaching books on the top shelves of the ceiling-high bookcases. In the corner, to the right of the beige couch: a big, old-fashioned desk, on top of which is a typewriter, a telephone, some books and papers; a swivel chair behind the desk; a smaller chair on the other side of the desk; nearby, a small blackboard.

The sequence begins with the camera panning to show the room. Rests finally on BAUER seated behind the desk in the swivel chair, typing. He is a handsome, dark-haired man in his middle or late forties, wearing a conservative business suit. Sound of footsteps (TOMAS entering the room). BAUER doesn't look up, continues typing. TOMAS comes into the shot: he approaches the desk hesitantly, then comes to a stop. BAUER raises his head for a second, then turns back to type a few more words. Finally BAUER looks up. He has intense eyes. He stands perfunctorily to greet TOMAS and shake hands with him, then sits down again.

9

BAUER

Sit down.

TOMAS sits in the smaller chair on the other side of the desk.

Medium shot: on TOMAS (from BAUER's point of view).

BAUER

(*Off*) I take it you are seriously interested in politics?

TOMAS

Yes.

BAUER

(*Off*) And you think you'll learn something working for me?

TOMAS

I hope so.

There is a pause. TOMAS, who probably hasn't admitted to himself until this moment how uncomfortable he is, looks away, then back at BAUER.

BAUER

(*Off*) Do you have a driver's license?

TOMAS

Yes.

BAUER

(*Off*) Do you smoke?

TOMAS nods.

Camera cuts back to BAUER, in medium shot, behind the desk.

10

BAUER

I trust you'll be careful about your cigarettes with all these papers around. There's a lifetime of work assembled in this room. I shouldn't like to see it all go up in smoke.

Two-shot of TOMAS and BAUER in profile seated at opposite sides of the desk. TOMAS is annoyed: BAUER isn't what he expected, too pompous and cold.

TOMAS

I'm careful.

BAUER

Good!

With this word BAUER smiles, evidently trying to change the mood and put TOMAS more at ease.

Medium close-up of BAUER. After looking at TOMAS for a moment, BAUER moves aside the typewriter and some of the papers to make a little space, and leans far over (looking straight into the camera), forearms on the desk and his chin almost touching the surface, in an exaggerated position of "confiding."

BAUER

Now then, where shall I begin? I suppose our mutual friend from Berlin has given you a general idea of the work . . .

Abruptly, BAUER sits upright, drums his fingers on the table.

BAUER

To begin with, you'll work chronologically, for the time being only on the materials prior to my arrival in Sweden. First, there are these papers—

BAUER points vaguely around the desk.

> BAUER
>
> —to read through and sort out. As you'll see,
> they are mostly letters from colleagues in the
> period 1945–47, just after the war. I imagine you'll
> recognize some of the names.

Medium close-up of TOMAS, who has taken out a pack
of cigarettes. He is, in fact, a heavy smoker.

Two-shot of BAUER and TOMAS in profile. BAUER grins.

> BAUER
>
> Smoke, by all means! . . . Then my journals of
> that period. They'll be somewhat harder . . .

BAUER has extended a heavy cigarette lighter and lit
TOMAS's cigarette while continuing to talk.

Close-up of the lighter in BAUER's hand as he sets it
down on the desk.

Back to the two-shot. BAUER notices TOMAS looking
at the lighter.

> BAUER
>
> Handsome, isn't it? Brecht gave it to me.

BAUER coughs, leans back in his chair, as if to cancel
the boast.

> BAUER
>
> Where was I? Yes, my journals. I have to explain
> to you the principles by which they can be dated

and the meaning of certain abbreviations I habit-
ually use . . .

He looks at TOMAS sharply. TOMAS is looking down,
his face slack.

> BAUER
> You're not paying attention!

BAUER stands. TOMAS looks up, annoyed.

> TOMAS
> Yes I am!

> BAUER
> Well, maybe we should leave the indexing of
> the journals for next week. Going through the
> letters will keep you busy for several days.

TOMAS has stood up, too.

TOMAS

Shall I start now?

BAUER

Certainly. You haven't anything else to do here, have you?

TOMAS grimaces. BAUER sits down.

BAUER

One more thing.

The tone is peremptory. TOMAS sits down, slowly. He shifts in his chair. BAUER looks at him.

BAUER

I needn't tell you, I hope, that your work here is absolutely confidential. There are many people who would give a good deal to know the contents of these papers. I intend to relieve their curiosity only when *I* am ready, and to give them as much information as *I* choose. Is that clear?

TOMAS is looking to his left (in the direction of the door), at something out of the frame. Footsteps.

TOMAS

Perfectly clear.

BAUER turns. A few seconds of the Wagner phrase.

Medium shot of FRANCESCA, partly in shadow, standing against the far wall. She is around thirty-five, small, has dark hair and large eyes; she wears a black dress. She looks both frightened and defiant.

Two-shot of TOMAS and BAUER again; TOMAS is still turned.

14

BAUER

(*To* TOMAS) Have you met my wife?

TOMAS stands up.

BAUER

(*To* FRANCESCA) Come, darling. Don't be shy.

Another shot of FRANCESCA. She seems to hesitate, but hasn't moved yet.

BAUER

(*Off*) This is Tomas. He's going to stay with us for a while.

FRANCESCA walks slowly across the room.

Camera back to BAUER and TOMAS. TOMAS smiles and extends his hand.

BAUER

Don't do that! She doesn't like to be touched.

TOMAS drops his hand.

Camera back to FRANCESCA, who is looking in TOMAS's direction, then turns to BAUER's.

Back to BAUER and TOMAS.

BAUER

It's best to pay no attention to her. It takes time for her to get accustomed to new people. But you'll see, if she likes you she can be quite friendly.

TOMAS looks from BAUER to FRANCESCA.

Back to FRANCESCA, who glares in BAUER's direction, then turns abruptly and goes to the window. From behind we

16

see her pick up a book on the windowsill and hurl it
through the window. Then she turns left and walks rapidly
out of the shot.

Sound of door slamming.

Another two-shot of TOMAS and BAUER. TOMAS leans in
alarm over the desk; BAUER, still sitting, looks down
pensively.

TOMAS
Is she ill?

BAUER

Not exactly. It's hard to explain. You'll have to be patient.

Shot of broken windowpane and curtain blowing in breeze from outside. Camera moves slowly down the window and rests on the broken glass on the sill.

BAUER

(*Off*) Would you clean up that glass before you get to work?

6. *Ingrid's room. Morning*

Medium shot of TOMAS (from behind): he is standing at the mirror, shaving. He has his shirt on. Sound of running water. INGRID (not in the shot) is speaking in the neutral "narrative" tone.

INGRID'S VOICE
"His wife's name is Francesca."

7. *Dining room of Bauer house. Evening*

The dining room has a fireplace, a long window framed by plants, prints of various species of fish on the walls, a large sideboard, and a long table with eight chairs.

The sequence starts with a long shot of the table: TOMAS,

FRANCESCA, and BAUER are at the far end, eating dinner. BAUER in the same suit as before, but with a napkin tucked under his chin; FRANCESCA in an elegant dress. TOMAS wears a jacket. BAUER has abominable table manners. He serves himself gross portions, wolfs down his food, talks with his mouth full, reaches across FRANCESCA's plate to drag a serving dish nearer to him, etc. Only BAUER is talking, but his mouth is so full his words are barely intelligible. The camera begins to track in as we hear TOMAS speaking part of the "narration."

> TOMAS'S VOICE
> "Bauer told me it might be necessary to live at the house for several weeks, because the initial cataloguing of his papers had to be done quickly."

The track ends in a medium shot of all three at the end of the table. So far we haven't seen either TOMAS or FRANCESCA speak. BAUER helps himself to still more food. Then, abruptly, he pushes back his chair, presses his napkin to his lips, then throws it down on the table, rises—making a choking sound—and rushes out of the room. TOMAS, startled, moves to follow him.

Medium shot of FRANCESCA.

> FRANCESCA
> Don't get up!

Camera back to TOMAS, who has frozen, halfway out of his seat. He sits down, surprised and pleased that she has spoken.

> TOMAS
> Perhaps he's ill.

Medium shot of FRANCESCA (TOMAS's point of view).

19

Her voice is cajoling now.

FRANCESCA

It's nothing, absolutely nothing. I've often seen him do that.

Medium close-up of TOMAS, who hesitantly begins to eat again. Sound of violent retching comes from the next room. TOMAS's fork stops in mid-air. He looks at FRANCESCA.

Camera back to FRANCESCA, who shakes her head firmly and smiles.

FRANCESCA

It's nothing. Believe me. Go on eating.

Long shot of that end of the room. TOMAS valiantly tries to go on eating. More disgusting retching sounds. Sound of toilet flushing. MRS. GRUNDBERG enters from the kitchen, bringing the dessert. She clears the table of the dinner plates, not reacting in any way to the noises BAUER is making.

Medium-long shot of TOMAS and FRANCESCA eating silently. Their eyes meet, TOMAS starts to smile, then freezes and looks down at the sound of a door opening, footsteps. BAUER comes into the frame, sits down again vigorously in his chair, tucks his napkin under his chin, and ladles several big helpings of fruit salad onto his plate.

Closer shot of the three. BAUER looks from one to the other, genially.

BAUER

I hope nothing has happened while I was gone.

FRANCESCA slams her fork down on the table in rage.

Darling, I was only teasing. Just a little joke.

BAUER winks conspiratorially at TOMAS, then shovels several heaping spoonfuls of whipped cream on his plate.

8. *Bauer library. That night*

Medium shot. TOMAS, fully dressed, his head propped up on a cushion, is dozing on the L-shaped couch near the fireplace. He has an open book in his hand. FRANCESCA, in a nightgown, half kneels on the couch, leaning toward him.

TOMAS'S VOICE
"I thought Francesca came into the library that night."

Close-up of TOMAS. He opens his eyes for a second, then turns his face away from her.

Medium shot: FRANCESCA leans over, and pulls at the cushion so that TOMAS's head rolls back toward her. TOMAS opens his eyes.

TOMAS
(*Whispering*) What do you want?

Close-up: FRANCESCA's hand descends to cover his mouth.

Long shot: FRANCESCA stands, crosses the room to the wall between the beige couch and the desk. Taking a key from her pocket, she unlocks a small square cupboard set in the wall. She steps aside. TOMAS comes into the shot, and stands just behind her. We see that the open cupboard holds a tape recorder. FRANCESCA puts the key into his hand, turns, and goes out of frame, leaving TOMAS standing there.

TOMAS'S VOICE
"She showed me a tape recorder."

9. *Bauer dining room. Next morning*

Medium-long shot. The room is bright with sunlight. TOMAS and BAUER are eating breakfast. BAUER in a suit, TOMAS in shirtsleeves. BAUER's plate is piled with his usual double portion. He butters himself several slices of toast. TOMAS is just picking at his food. BAUER glances at TOMAS, and speaks with his mouth full.

BAUER

More toast?

TOMAS shakes his head.

TOMAS

No, thanks.

BAUER

I'd like you to take Francesca for a stroll this morning. She's been ill a long time and hardly ever leaves the house, since I've no time to accompany her.

BAUER continues eating in his usual fashion. TOMAS, who has finished, wipes his mouth; then lights a cigarette.

TOMAS

But shouldn't I be working all day? You said the work was urgent.

BAUER

This is more important. The work can wait.

Shot of the underside of the table. Whining noise. A dog is sniffing at BAUER's and TOMAS's shoes. BAUER's hand comes down with a piece of bacon. The dog snaps it from him.

10. *From the top of the tallest building in central Stockholm. Day*

Camera pans over the city, coming to rest on the apartment building where INGRID and TOMAS live. Noise of cars, boat whistles.

11. *Ingrid's roof, room. Same day*

Long shot down the roof outside INGRID's room. Continuation of natural sounds in preceding sequence. INGRID and TOMAS come around the chimney into the shot. INGRID in a sweater, woolen skirt, and high boots. TOMAS in jeans and a leather jacket. They have obviously been pacing about on the roof for some time, and quarreling. They walk slowly toward the camera, talking. We hear the agitated tone but can't make out the words until they come much closer. INGRID slows down and says plaintively:

                    INGRID
        We hardly ever see each other.

TOMAS is bending over, tying one of his shoelaces. He looks up irritably.

                    TOMAS
        Don't start that again!

He finishes tying his shoe. Then, without looking back,

goes to the window, bends over to get through, and jumps down into the room.

Change of shot (camera, still on the roof, now faces the window).

INGRID, disconsolate, slowly walks across to the window and leans against it, not looking in. She is in the middle ground of the shot; in the background of the shot we see TOMAS, inside the room, busy at the kitchen area.

Medium shot (camera is inside the room now): TOMAS at the stove. He looks up.

> TOMAS
> Want to eat something?

INGRID answers sullenly.

> INGRID
> (*Off*) I've already eaten.

Change of shot. The noise of someone jumping down. The camera starts on TOMAS still at the kitchen area, then pans with him as he walks over to the table, carrying plates, bread, jam. The camera stops when it picks up INGRID, who is now just inside the room, by the window, leaning against the wall.

> INGRID
> I don't see why you have to live there.

Camera continues panning to pick up TOMAS, now seated on an orange crate at the table, spreading jam on the bread.

> TOMAS
> That's what Bauer wants. It's only for a little while.

TOMAS rises and goes toward the kitchen area. The camera pans with him; stops again on INGRID, still standing by the window.

INGRID

But what do you *do* there all day?

TOMAS comes back into the shot, carrying some butter.

Camera pans with him as he returns to the table and starts eating.

TOMAS

Lots of things. There's always something to do.

Pan back to INGRID.

INGRID

Oh, I wish you hadn't taken this job!

Camera follows INGRID as she comes over to the table. They are both in the shot now. Standing, she begins buttering a slice of bread. Reaching for the jam, she inadvertently knocks a plate off the table. Sharp noise of plate breaking. TOMAS jumps.

INGRID

For God's sake, what's the matter with you?

TOMAS

All this mess gets on my nerves.

INGRID's voice becomes shriller.

INGRID

The plate?

TOMAS waves his arm.

26

TOMAS

No, everything! Can't you clean the place up while I'm gone.

Medium shot of INGRID, whose tone has suddenly softened.

INGRID

It's our mess. I like it . . . It makes me think of you.

Two-shot: INGRID and TOMAS. TOMAS looks at her stiffly, then grins. A slice of bread still in hand, he gets up, goes around the table and hugs her, laughing.

TOMAS

Idiot!

She resists his embrace a little, then after a moment returns it. Holding each other and laughing together, they turn around several times. Each holds a slice of bread in one hand, beyond the shoulder of the other.

12. *Bauer library. Early afternoon, several days later*

Medium shot of TOMAS, wearing jeans and a shirt, sitting at the desk in BAUER's place. He's making neat stacks of the notebooks. Finds one of a different size at the bottom of an unsorted pile, and tosses it into a wooden box on the floor to his right. Then he leans back in the swivel chair, looks around. He lights a cigarette with the Brecht lighter. TOMAS is a heavy smoker; there is a big ashtray on the desk now, filled with cigarette butts.

He thumbs through some more papers, makes some entries in a notebook. Stops. He inhales on his cigarette. Then

reaches into a pocket and takes out the little key. Rises, goes to the wall cupboard and unlocks it, lifts out the tape recorder. He sets it on top of the desk. Still standing, he stares down at it.

Closer shot: TOMAS tentatively presses the "play" button, then leans back against the wall. We hear snatches of music, the sound of machine-gun fire, a crowd chanting, then BAUER's voice.

BAUER

(*Recorded*) I can feel the disease getting worse. The doctors promised me at least two years—maybe as long as four—but I suspect they were wrong. I already have symptoms that shouldn't have appeared for another six months. . . . What wor-

ries me most is how Francesca will survive me.
Who will look after her? And my political . . .

Here BAUER's voice is drowned out by sound of rifle fire
that had started up faintly in the middle of the passage.

Sound of a noise coming from outside the room. TOMAS
looks up, hastily switches off the tape recorder, returns it
to the cupboard and closes and locks the door, pockets
the key, and pivots just in time.

Long shot (from TOMAS's point of view). BAUER opens the
door and stands on the threshold. He is wearing an overcoat, scarf, gloves, and dark glasses. His face and tone
are impassive.

I'll be out for several hours. I expect you to keep my wife company.

Medium shot of TOMAS, immobile with surprise and relief. Sound of receding footsteps.

TOMAS'S VOICE

"This time I couldn't think of any reasons for objecting."

13. *Living room of Bauer house. The same afternoon, later*

A long, pleasant, elegant room. Sofa, two end tables with lamps, a coffee table, two dark brown upholstered chairs, a small bookcase, a mahogany cabinet, paintings, a wall clock, and a mirror.

The sequence starts with a medium shot of TOMAS, standing with his back to a large landscape painting which fills the whole frame. He holds a book and, after a shy glance and a second's further hesitation, starts reading aloud. As he reads, he paces back and forth in front of the painting, coming in and out of the shot on both sides.

TOMAS

Fourth Canto . . . 'Between two foods, equally near and equally tempting, a free man would die of hunger before he brought either to his lips. So a lamb, between ravenous wolves, would stand in equal fear of both. So would a hound stand between two deer. Therefore if I kept silence, urged equally by my doubts, I neither blame nor commend myself, since it was of necessity. I was silent,

but my desire was painted on my face, and with it
my question, far more warmly than in plain
words . . .'

Throughout this first image of the sequence, the audience
doesn't know where we are and doesn't get any sense
of the living room until the next shot—a long shot of
FRANCESCA stretched out on the sofa on her right side,
wearing a stylish short dress ornamented with sequins.
She interrupts TOMAS to recite from memory in Italian
the same passage from Dante's *Paradiso*. She closes her
eyes as she starts, opens them at "*Io mi tacea.*"

FRANCESCA
Intra due cibi, distanti e moventi
d'un modo, prima si morria di fame,
che liber'uomo l'un recasse ai denti;
sí si starebbe un agno intra due brame
di fieri lupi, egualmente temendo;
sí si starebbe un cane intra due dame:
per che, s' i' mi tacea, me non riprendo,
dalli miei dubbi d'un modo sospinto,
poich'era necessario, nè commendo.
Io mi tacea, ma 'l mio disir dipinto
m'era nel viso, e 'l domandar con ello,
più caldo assai che per parlar distinto.

During the last lines TOMAS has entered the shot from the
right, crossing in front of FRANCESCA. Looking down at her,
he speaks softly, as if afraid of breaking a spell.

TOMAS
Go on.

FRANCESCA shakes her head, smiles at him. TOMAS sits down

31

slowly in an upholstered chair very near the sofa and reluctantly takes up the book again.

TOMAS
'I see well how you are drawn by both desires—'

He breaks off abruptly, at the sound of the front door opening and closing, turns around. FRANCESCA abruptly sits up.

Long shot of BAUER, who has returned. He stands in the center of the living room. He's still wearing his coat, scarf, and gloves.

BAUER
Did you have a good time?

Back to the preceding shot.

TOMAS
I'll get back to work now.

TOMAS leans over to put the book back in the low bookcase, stands up.

Back to the shot of BAUER. As he talks, BAUER removes his gloves and scarf.

BAUER
Were there any phone calls for me, Tomas?

TOMAS, who has to pass him to get out of the living room, comes into the shot.

TOMAS
None.

BAUER holds out his clothing with his left arm, but doesn't

32

take his eyes off TOMAS. FRANCESCA, who has also risen, now passes briefly through the shot, taking BAUER's coat, etc., without looking at him. She leaves the room.

> BAUER
>
> That's peculiar. I'm expecting a very important call from Argentina. You're sure you were here all the time?

TOMAS is standing close to BAUER now, waiting for the questions to end so he can leave the room.

> TOMAS
>
> Right in this room.

> BAUER
>
> And with enough attention left from your activities with my wife to hear the phone if it happened to ring?

TOMAS glares with rage at BAUER.

14. *Bauer house: living room and hallway. Evening*

Long shot; the camera is stationed behind the wooden grill that partly separates the living room from the dining room. BAUER and four other middle-aged men, all wearing dark business suits, occupy the couch and three chairs drawn up near it at the far end of the living room. They are leaning close together, talking conspiratorially.

Cut to a closer shot from inside the living room. Camera on MRS. GRUNDBERG, who has entered, carrying a tray with a bottle of cognac and glasses. Sound of rattling glassware (her hands tremble slightly). Camera pans with her as she

approaches the men. At first BAUER doesn't notice her, but as she begins to set the tray down on the coffee table, BAUER looks up angrily and waves her away. She hesitates for a moment, then puts down the tray firmly, turns and starts to walk out of the room. Camera pans back with her a little way, enough to see her halt for a second and make an annoyed grimace over her shoulder in the direction of BAUER.

Cut to the threshold between the hallway and dining room, near the wooden grille. FRANCESCA is standing there, just out of sight of the men in the living room, and evidently watching them. A moment later TOMAS passes behind her in the hallway. She turns and pulls him toward her, whispering.

> FRANCESCA
> Do you know who's here tonight?

TOMAS shakes his head.

> FRANCESCA
> We musn't disturb them. It's a meeting.

She takes TOMAS's hand.

> FRANCESCA
> Take me for a drive.

TOMAS is startled.

> TOMAS
> Now? Where do you want to go?

> FRANCESCA
> Anywhere. Just to get out of the house.

She takes his arm and they pass into the hallway.

15. *Exterior of the Bauer house. Minutes later*

Long shot (camera is across the street) of TOMAS and FRANCESCA hurrying through the gate. FRANCESCA is dragging her coat on the ground. The dog runs after them. The sound of the front door opening; voices. They stop a few feet short of the car, which is parked on the street, and

35

FRANCESCA presses against TOMAS, whispering hoarsely. She seems terrified.

> FRANCESCA
> Too late! They're leaving.

> BAUER
> (*Off*) Francesca? Are you out there?

> FRANCESCA
> Don't say anything!

She turns abruptly and rushes back through the gate, leaving TOMAS standing on the street looking in the direction she has gone.

16. Bauer library. Late that night

Medium close-up of TOMAS asleep on the beige couch. BAUER leans over him and tugs hard at his shoulder.

> BAUER
> She's locked herself in the car! You must help me. I'm afraid she may do herself harm.

BAUER seems in a state of violent panic.

Medium-long shot of the two. TOMAS, half asleep, doesn't understand.

> TOMAS
> What?

> BAUER
> I want you to talk to her! Tell her to open the door!

TOMAS sits up wearily, coughs.

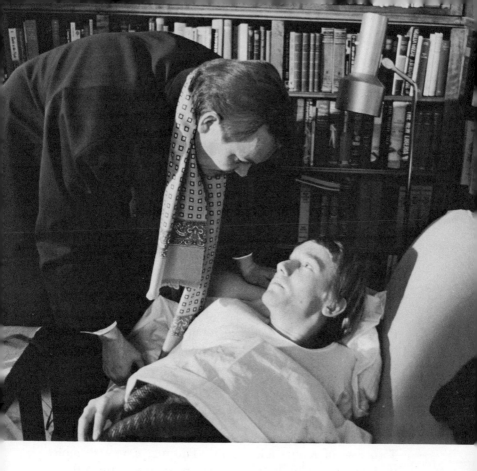

17. *Exterior of Bauer house. Minutes later*

Long shot of the rear of the house. BAUER, followed
by TOMAS, comes through the back kitchen door and
walks swiftly along the path to the garage. TOMAS follows
behind him, still sleepy and coughing, zipping up the
leather jacket he has hurriedly put on over his T-shirt
and pants. The camera pans (we are behind them now):
They go through the rear door of the garage.

Closer shot, from the threshold of the garage. The front of the car faces the camera (the headlights are on). FRANCESCA, wearing a fur coat, is in the driver's seat. BAUER rushes to the right side of the car. He motions urgently to FRANCESCA to come out, pulls at the locked door, then turns hysterically toward TOMAS.

BAUER

Do something! Can't you do something?

TOMAS stands next to BAUER. We see FRANCESCA looking impassively from one to the other. Then she starts the windshield wipers. BAUER grips TOMAS's arm.

A long shot from behind the car. FRANCESCA switches off the windshield wipers and starts the motor. BAUER throws himself between the moving car and the garage wall. FRANCESCA slams down on the brakes, stopping the car just before it hits him.

Another shot (again from the front) of FRANCESCA in the car: she smiles at BAUER, leans over, and opens the right door.

Two-shot of BAUER and TOMAS. Panting, BAUER stumbles past TOMAS, who hasn't moved from the right side of the car.

BAUER

I'm sorry. It's a mistake. Go back to bed.

BAUER grabs the door, gets inside, and slams it shut. He begins to embrace FRANCESCA passionately, while FRANCESCA, a fixed smile on her face, gazes through the window at TOMAS.

Medium shot of TOMAS, who remains beside the car,

38

watching. Wagner phrase starts and continues to the end of the sequence.

Back to frontal shot of the car. BAUER is hunched over FRANCESCA, his head in her lap. FRANCESCA reaches into the glove compartment, takes out a spray can. Still looking at TOMAS, she begins to spray the inside of the window with a thick white foam.

Medium shot of TOMAS, staring in the direction of the car. He looks cold: his shoulders are hunched and both hands are in his jacket pockets.

Back to the car (same shot as before). Now the entire front window is coated from the inside with opaque white foam.

18. A cafeteria. Afternoon

The sequence begins with a frontal close-up of an OLD MAN talking gibberish to himself. He has a stubbly beard and one can tell from his collar alone that he must be wearing old, soiled clothes.

TOMAS
(Off) What's he saying?

A medium-long shot shows where we are now: a crowded cafeteria. INGRID and TOMAS are in the foreground of the shot, seated opposite each other at a small table, drinking coffee. INGRID has on a mod vinyl dress and high boots; TOMAS wears the usual jeans and sweater. The crazy OLD MAN is alone at the next table (the background in this shot). He is messing with a sandwich and some layer cake and continuing to jabber: he seems to be complaining about his food. As the OLD MAN gets louder and bolder in his gestures, people at adjacent tables start paying more attention to him. INGRID glances at the OLD MAN, then turns back to TOMAS. She looks tired, and rubs her eyes.

INGRID
Nothing. Go on with what you were telling me.

TOMAS

That's all. Just what I've told you. He's got some fatal disease. At least, he believes he has. But I'm not sure. He's full of fantasies of persecution and disaster. The exile's mentality, I suppose . . .

TOMAS, visibly nervous, toys with a matchbook or shreds a napkin as he talks. When INGRID impatiently takes it from him, he doesn't react.

TOMAS

About her, I know even less. I don't understand what's between them.

Medium shot of the OLD MAN at his table, grunting, gesticulating, messing with his food and his battered hat, alternately self-absorbed and addressing people at nearby tables. A WAITRESS comes over and speaks politely.

WAITRESS

Would you be a little quieter? Otherwise you'll have to leave.

The OLD MAN sticks out his tongue at her and makes a disgusting noise. Unable to handle the situation, she backs off.

Two-shot of INGRID and TOMAS. TOMAS has watched the moment with the WAITRESS. He looks at INGRID.

> TOMAS
>
> There are too many crazy people in the world. Let's get out of here.

> INGRID
>
> Just ignore him.

> TOMAS
>
> I can't.

Medium shot of INGRID. The expression on her face is at once bitter, sly, and vulnerable.

> INGRID
>
> I'm not impressed by your Arthur Bauer.

Two-shot of INGRID and TOMAS.

> TOMAS
>
> No?

> INGRID
>
> Is she very attractive?

> TOMAS
>
> Don't be silly.

> INGRID
>
> I'm not being silly. I'm just trying to understand what I feel about all this.

Medium-long shot of the OLD MAN. He is becoming louder and even more grotesque. After a few moments, the MANAGER of the cafeteria—a burly man around fifty— comes to his table and addresses him firmly.

You'll have to go.

Although the OLD MAN howls and tries to resist, the MANAGER without much difficulty picks him up from his chair by the collar and starts pushing him toward the door. TOMAS abruptly signals the WAITRESS for the check.

19. The street. Two minutes later

In long shot, we see INGRID and TOMAS leaving the restaurant; they turn down the street, coming toward the camera. We can see, though at first they can't, that the CRAZY OLD MAN (in the foreground of the shot) is huddled in the next doorway. As they pass him, he jumps out and grabs at TOMAS's jacket, yelling something incomprehensible. TOMAS shouts at him and pushes him away. Camera pans to show TOMAS and INGRID from behind, walking away. The OLD MAN follows them at a safe distance down the street, shouting and shaking his fist.

20. Bauer library. Morning

Long shot: TOMAS is sitting, yoga position, on the beige couch, looking over some manuscripts and making notes in a loose-leaf binder. Several times he consults some of the papers piled on the table in front of the couch. After some moments of what seems complete absorption in the work, he stops, leans back, lights a cigarette.

Sighs, puts out the cigarette, stands. He goes to the wall cupboard, unlocks the door, and lifts out the tape recorder, which he places on the table in front of the couch.

Close-up of tape recorder. TOMAS's hand enters the frame and presses the "play" button. Confused sounds: marching, cheers, applause.

Camera pans up to rest on a wall of books. Gradually, BAUER's voice becomes audible. He's speaking in a low, confidential tone.

> BAUER
> (*Recorded*) There is so little time left and I have so much to do. My worry about Francesca is interfering with my political work . . .

At this point the tape becomes noisily inaudible.

Another close-up of the tape recorder. We see TOMAS's finger pushing "off."

21. *Road in front of Bauer house. Day*

Long shot. TOMAS and BAUER standing beside the BAUER car. BAUER, who wears a broad black hat, ceremoniously hands TOMAS a manila envelope and the car keys.

> TOMAS'S VOICE
> "He asked me to transmit a highly confidential message to someone."

Closer two-shot of TOMAS and BAUER.

BAUER

All you have to do is deliver this envelope. There's
no risk in it for you. It's simply at this moment
I can't trust any conventional means of sending
it. You remember exactly what I told you?

TOMAS shifts restlessly from foot to foot.

TOMAS

Yes.

BAUER

The car? Color, make, license number?

TOMAS

Yes.

TOMAS moves to open the car door.

BAUER

One more thing. I want you to wear this hat.

Another two-shot (still closer). BAUER produces another
hat like the one he's wearing. TOMAS stares at it, smiles
derisively.

TOMAS

You must be joking!

BAUER holds the hat out to him.

BAUER

Not at all.

TOMAS

What is it, a signal?

BAUER

You could call it that.

46

Medium-long shot. TOMAS shrugs his shoulders, puts on the hat. Opens the car door and gets in. BAUER leans over to give him some final instructions, which we can't hear.

22. Underground garage. An hour later

Medium shot taken from the back seat of the BAUER car. TOMAS is at the wheel, driving slowly down the ramp (Level C). The car turns the corner.

Another medium shot from the hood of the car: TOMAS, full-face, through the window. His face is expressionless.

A brief long shot of a man in a long trenchcoat, partly hidden by the parked cars, running along the wall. The camera is at the far wall.

Long shot: we see the car and TOMAS in profile. TOMAS slows down to pull alongside an American car parked in the middle of a line of small European cars. He throws the manila envelope through the right front open window of his car onto the front seat of the American car.

Long shot. We see TOMAS from behind, continuing down the ramp. The camera holds until his car is out of sight.

No natural sounds (e.g., the car motor) in this sequence, except for the footsteps of the running man. A passage from Mahler's Tenth Symphony over the whole sequence.

23. *Ingrid's room. Night*

Long shot: INGRID is in bed. Sounds: the door being unlocked, footsteps. TOMAS enters the shot and stands by the bed, looking down at INGRID. She opens her eyes.

> INGRID
>
> Why are you wearing that awful hat?

TOMAS takes off the hat, tosses it on the floor. Without looking at her, he undresses. She watches him, then speaks sarcastically.

> INGRID
>
> Did you get tonight off?

Naked, TOMAS joins her in bed. They lie side by side without speaking for a moment.

> TOMAS
>
> They went to bed early. I just left.

He turns toward INGRID, wanting to make love. INGRID doesn't. He lies on his back again.

> TOMAS
>
> What's wrong?

> INGRID
>
> Nothing.

TOMAS sits up, takes a cigarette from the nighttable, lights it, puts the ashtray in his lap.

> TOMAS
>
> Listen, if my working for Bauer—

INGRID

It's not that!

He touches her shoulder. She pulls away.

TOMAS

Don't be angry.

INGRID

Let's go to sleep.

INGRID turns on her left side (away from him), then her stomach, trying to settle into a comfortable position. It doesn't work. Irritably she returns to lying on her back, then reaches over and takes TOMAS's cigarette from him. He lights another one, inhales, coughs.

TOMAS

I want to stop smoking.

He stubs out the cigarette.

INGRID

Then why don't you?

TOMAS

A question of stronger and weaker forces, isn't it?

He looks at her. She's looking straight ahead.

INGRID

I didn't know you were such a great believer in the power of the will.

She gives him her cigarette, then turns on her side, away from him, to sleep. He starts smoking it.

Outside, night. Very long shot of a black car driving along the street in front of the apârtment building. The car's headlights pick up the row of parked, empty cars. The car is moving very slowly. It's too dark—and the distance too great between the camera and the car—to see the driver.

Back in the apartment. Long shot. TOMAS and INGRID are sleeping. Silence. Then, sound of a car's screeching brakes, a muffled crash, breaking glass. TOMAS is awakened by the noise. He gets out of bed, goes to the far window, looks down. Turns back to the bed. Wagner phrase starts up, continues to the end of the sequence.

Long shot of the bed (from TOMAS's point of view). FRANCESCA, naked, is lying there, looking at him.

Close-up of FRANCESCA. White dissolve. [Only two shots in the film end with a dissolve.]

Camera tracks behind TOMAS as he returns to the bed. FRANCESCA, smiling, reaches up for him. As he lies on top of her, she pulls up the sheet to cover them completely.

24. Ingrid's room. The next morning

Medium shot. Sunlight. TOMAS stands before the stove, cracking eggs into the frying pan. He looks over his shoulder.

Long shot of the bed (from TOMAS's point of view). INGRID is lying on her stomach, still asleep.

Another shot of TOMAS at the stove (his back to the camera this time). He is taking the eggs out of the frying pan with a spatula.

50

INGRID'S VOICE
"I pleaded with him not to go back."

25. *Exterior of Bauer house. Later that morning*

Long shot. TOMAS comes up the flagstone walk. He's
wearing corduroy pants and the leather jacket. As he
turns the corner of the walk, we see BAUER raking leaves
about thirty feet in front of the house. He scowls as
soon as he sees TOMAS and throws down the rake. His
voice is very severe.

> BAUER
>
> There you are! Do you want this job or not?
> If so, you must understand that you're required
> to stay here. At any moment I may have work for
> you, or my wife may need you.

TOMAS stands near BAUER, defiant, not answering.

> BAUER
>
> You *have* come here to work, haven't you?

> TOMAS
>
> What are you talking about? What else?

BAUER's tone changes.

> BAUER
>
> You're not a spy in my house, are you? You know
> I have many enemies. And people have many
> disguises.

BAUER removes his dark glasses, then puts them back on.

BAUER

Don't glasses change my appearance?

TOMAS

Not particularly.

BAUER

Look again.

Close-up of TOMAS's face: he looks suddenly agitated.

Medium close-up of BAUER's face, which looks at first intent and curious, then softer.

BAUER

Well, I'm willing to let you off this time . . . But you'll have to speak to Francesca and convince her that it's all right.

Medium-long shot of both.

TOMAS

Where is she?

BAUER motions with his head toward the house. TOMAS starts up the walk. BAUER picks up the rake and begins raking the leaves again, whistling.

26. *Bauer living room. Several minutes later*

TOMAS enters. The camera follows him, showing FRANCESCA, wearing the black dress again, sitting in a big chair. She has laid out a game of solitaire on the coffee table. He goes over to her.

TOMAS

Francesca?

She ignores him. Her expression is severe. He squats beside her, touches her shoulder. She pulls away sharply. He stays there a moment, watching her play; then moves a card for her. Angrily, she sweeps up the cards. Sound of heavy footsteps.

Long shot from the other side of the room. BAUER enters—
he's in the back of the shot—and comes forward. TOMAS
stands.

> BAUER

What have you both decided?

> TOMAS

Nothing. You're right. She *is* angry.

> BAUER

Well, that's easy to cure.

BAUER goes over and slaps FRANCESCA's face. TOMAS tries
to restrain him. BAUER shoves him away.

> BAUER

Don't you dare interfere! This is between my
wife and me.

> TOMAS

I'm not going to stand by here and watch you—

> BAUER

Why not? Why shouldn't you watch something
you don't understand? Now, watch!

Two-shot: BAUER and FRANCESCA. BAUER slaps her again.

> FRANCESCA

Tomas!

> BAUER

You see, now she's talking to you. It's really quite
simple to manage these things if you know how.

Long shot again (same as before): BAUER leaves the
room.

Two-shot: FRANCESCA and TOMAS. Mortified, appalled,

TOMAS at first doesn't look at FRANCESCA. Then he holds out his hand; she takes it, smiles.

TOMAS
I don't know what to say.

FRANCESCA
Don't say anything.

TOMAS
Is he listening outside?

FRANCESCA
Why do you ask that?

Tracking shot. FRANCESCA gets up, crosses the room to a mirror, examines her face. TOMAS follows her, stands to one side of the mirror.

TOMAS
Doesn't he frighten you?

FRANCESCA laughs.

FRANCESCA
Of course not. He's the dearest, kindest man in the world.

Simultaneously, BAUER is calling from outside the room.

BAUER
(Off) Tomas, would you please come into the library? I have work for you.

TOMAS moves behind FRANCESCA while she does something with her hair.

TOMAS
Are you all right?

FRANCESCA turns toward him, nods.

TOMAS

You're sure?

FRANCESCA nods again. She straightens his collar, puts
her hand on his hair, and slightly leans against him,
her face close to his. TOMAS almost kisses her, then
lowers his head.

Another two-shot.

FRANCESCA

You don't like me.

TOMAS

(*Almost laughing*) You're wrong. I do like you.

FRANCESCA sees the confusion in his face, and laughs.
Now she seems much more animated.

FRANCESCA
Then read to me.

TOMAS
What shall I read?

She takes his arm.

FRANCESCA
The same thing you were reading the other day.

They walk toward the sofa.

Camera on TOMAS, who takes the book from the bookshelf. He sits down slowly on the couch and, self-consciously, starts reading.

TOMAS
'I see well how you are drawn by both desires, so
that your eagerness itself is bound up and stifled.
You reason, "If the right will endures, how can another person's violence lessen the measure of my
merit?"—'

FRANCESCA
(*Off*) Io veggio ben come ti tira
uno ed altro disio, sì che tua cura
sè stessa lega sì che fuor non spira.
Tu argomenti: Se 'l buon voler dura,
la violenza altrui per qual ragione
di meritar mi scema la misura?

FRANCESCA, who is also on the couch, leans over (into the shot) and takes the book from his hands.

TOMAS

What is it?

FRANCESCA

I've changed my mind.

TOMAS

What do you want to do?

Close-up of FRANCESCA.

FRANCESCA

Let's make believe. I'm a princess in an enchanted castle, and—

TOMAS

(*Off*) —I've come to rescue you?

FRANCESCA smiles.

FRANCESCA

Don't be silly . . . Now let me see . . . What should you wear?

FRANCESCA gets up suddenly and goes out of the shot.

Two-shot of TOMAS and FRANCESCA. TOMAS is standing. FRANCESCA puts a false beard on TOMAS, then looks at him quizzically.

FRANCESCA

No, that's not right.

She goes to a cedar chest, opens a drawer, takes out a roll of gauze. She stands on a chair; TOMAS stands before her, "at attention." She bandages TOMAS's head.

Sound of the wall clock striking eleven. Then she kisses TOMAS on the mouth. She pushes him away playfully. He takes a few steps, then turns around as "Frankenstein's monster"—and begins to approach her. She cries out in mock-fright. He chases her around the coffee table twice. They fall partly on the couch, laughing hysterically, embracing.

MRS. GRUNDBERG enters, makes a signal to FRANCESCA. FRANCESCA sits up and whispers to TOMAS.

FRANCESCA

He's calling me. I'll be right back.

TOMAS slides down to the floor; sits, head down.

BAUER enters, crosses the room almost at a run. TOMAS tries to get up, but BAUER holds him down.

BAUER

Wait! She'll be back in a minute. I must tell you something while she can't hear us . . .

TOMAS stops struggling, inclines his head forward.

BAUER

(*Whispering*) It's the food. I'm afraid the food is—

Sound of footsteps. FRANCESCA stands in the doorway. She looks angry.

FRANCESCA

What are you two whispering about?

Long shot from in back of the couch: BAUER and TOMAS in the foreground, seen from behind; FRANCESCA in the background. BAUER stands. Suddenly his voice is entirely different—ingratiating.

BAUER

Nothing, darling. Tomas was telling me about your little game.

TOMAS stands up, starts unwinding the bandage. BAUER suddenly seems furious.

TOMAS

If you'll excuse me . . .

BAUER

Just a minute. I think Tomas owes me an explanation . . .

TOMAS

Explanation of what?

BAUER

Of what you have done with my wife.

TOMAS

What I've done with her! The question is what *you've* done with her.

BAUER

You think I don't know you've already slept together. Last night, for instance.

TOMAS

Last night, as you perfectly well know, I wasn't
even here. Are you telling me your wife wasn't here
either?

BAUER

Oh, she was here . . . But maybe you were here,
too. Maybe you sneaked in and out.

TOMAS

I've had enough of this. I quit. You and your
manuscripts can go to hell!

TOMAS moves toward the end of the room.

Medium shot of all three. FRANCESCA is standing there,
holding out another pair of dark glasses. BAUER suddenly
becomes ingratiating.

BAUER

You can't quit now. See, it's all a game. Come
on, my boy, humor me. And can't you see that
Francesca wants you to stay? Stay . . . if not
for my sake, then for hers.

Closer shot: TOMAS and FRANCESCA. FRANCESCA fits the
sunglasses on TOMAS's face. Wagner phrase.

27. *Bauer library. Afternoon*

TOMAS is alone, working at the desk, smoking. We hear

the dog barking. BAUER enters, sits down wearily on the beige couch. He picks up a copy of *Neue Zuricher Zeitung*, starts to read it, realizes he's not wearing his glasses, feels for them in his jacket pocket, discovers he doesn't have them with him, sighs, puts the newspaper down on the table. He looks over at TOMAS, who has continued working since BAUER entered the room, and not once looked at him.

BAUER

How is it going?

TOMAS gives BAUER a tiny, blank glance and answers tonelessly.

TOMAS

All right, except for the gaps in the notebooks from 1953 that I mentioned to you.

BAUER

Show me.

TOMAS brings him the loose-leaf binder. Then sits down stiffly on the edge of the table in front of the couch. He doesn't look at BAUER.

BAUER

I don't know what ever possessed me to undertake this project . . . Reviewing one's whole life is a formidable task. And there are so many secrets I can't reveal.

Closer shot of the two. BAUER looks extremely tired. He appears to be talking to himself.

BAUER

And Francesca. What am I to do with her? That weighs on me so . . .

With these last words, TOMAS looks at BAUER. There are tears in BAUER's eyes. BAUER suddenly seems aware of TOMAS, and looks at him in an ingratiating way.

> BAUER
>
> But you've been a great help, Tomas. It's a relief to have you here.

New shot: camera further away.

> TOMAS
>
> Exactly what is the matter with her?

BAUER stands, goes over to the desk. His back is to TOMAS now.

> BAUER
>
> If only you could have known her a few years ago! She was so different then. . . . And when we were first married, you can't imagine what she was like. So lively and loving. . . . But now . . .

BAUER looks over at TOMAS sadly. TOMAS gazes at him, incredulous.

> BAUER
>
> Oh, I know you think I'm harsh with her. But when you get to know her better . . .

BAUER sighs. Then moves to far side of desk, looks back at TOMAS.

> BAUER
>
> A great love is an enormous responsibility. . . . Are you in love, Tomas?

TOMAS stands up, moves toward BAUER without meeting his look.

TOMAS

I don't know. I think so.

BAUER

Think so? There's no "thinking so" when one is really in love . . .

28. *Library, garden of Bauer house. A little later*

TOMAS at work. He seems restless. After a moment, he gets up, goes to the window.

Shot, through the window (TOMAS's point of view) of BAUER alone, pacing up and down in the garden; he comes in and out of the frame.

Shot, from behind, of TOMAS at the window.

> TOMAS'S VOICE
> "I pitied him. Despite his arrogance . . ."

Camera outside. BAUER, sitting in a swing, is calling the dog (who is out of frame). His voice and manner are exaggeratedly cajoling.

> BAUER
> Come here! Come here!

Loud, vicious barking. BAUER looks miserable. He slumps over.

29. Bauer library. Somewhat later

With a furtive air, TOMAS unlocks the cupboard and takes out the tape recorder. Puts it on the far end of the table before the couch, kneels down on the floor in front of it. He presses the "play" button.

At first all we hear is static. TOMAS leans forward. He presses another button, to move to another part of the tape—trying to find a clear section. Now we hear the sound of bombs exploding, very loud. Then BAUER's voice, speaking softly.

> BAUER
> (*Recorded*) I've decided to do away with Francesca. There's no point in my keeping her alive any more. It pains me, but—

TOMAS settles back on his heels. BAUER's voice dissolves into a German political song.

30. Drottninggatan. Day

Long shot: the street, fairly crowded. TOMAS and FRANCESCA come toward the camera. TOMAS is taking FRANCESCA for a walk. She is wearing a fur coat. He looks frequently at her, she gazes stonily ahead.

> TOMAS
>
> Why so silent today? You needn't be afraid of me.

> FRANCESCA
>
> I'm not afraid of you.

Camera pans with them as they continue walking.

31. Östermalm subway station. An hour later

Two-shot of TOMAS and FRANCESCA, walking along the platform, waiting for a train. There is hardly anyone else in the station. FRANCESCA is still being completely remote. TOMAS lights a cigarette, FRANCESCA takes it from his mouth and throws it on the tracks. He smiles slightly and puts his arm around her. Camera tracks over section of Siri Derkert murals on the walls (Fanon, Brecht, etc.).

Medium shot of TOMAS, with a section of the wall in focus behind him.

> TOMAS
>
> There's something so innocent about this art. It almost makes me believe in nonviolence and in human goodness.

66

More details of the station: the names and images on the walls, peace emblems on the floor.

A new shot of the two, standing by an undecorated part of the wall.

FRANCESCA

Will you kill my husband?

She opens her purse, offers him a revolver. TOMAS stares at her incredulously, then turns and walks away.

TOMAS'S VOICE
"She gave me a revolver."

FRANCESCA follows TOMAS. She holds out the revolver. He refuses it. Train comes into the station. We can see them talking animatedly but don't hear what they say. They board the train together.

32. Ingrid's room. Day

Medium-long shot: INGRID is slouched in the comfortable chair, legs dangling over one arm, reading. She turns a page of the book.

Medium close-up, from over INGRID's shoulder, of the book she is reading. She turns back to the title page; it is a book by Arthur Bauer, *Die Revolution und Seine Feinde*. Opposite the title page is a full-page photograph of BAUER.

Another frontal shot of INGRID. She closes the book, puts it down, stares into space. Over this last shot of the sequence we hear INGRID's voice.

INGRID'S VOICE
"Ho Chi Minh said that all people are good, only governments are bad . . . No . . . All quotations are good, only people are bad."

33. Bedroom in Bauer house. Night

Long shot of BAUER pacing back and forth in the small

alcove which serves as a dressing room; he keeps returning to a wall mirror to squint at himself. He wears a dressing gown and leather slippers.

BAUER

> In an age of revolutions, the only adequate profession is that of the revolutionary.

Shot change. BAUER sits down at the dressing table and looks at himself in this mirror. Camera is behind him.

BAUER

> Consider the two basic principles of this society. The commodity and the spectacle.

He takes out a hairpiece, tries it on, frowns, takes it off. Makes several faces at himself in the mirror. Then his expression goes blank again.

BAUER

> In my profession, it is often necessary to disguise oneself.

BAUER begins to dab stuff on his chin. He is going to put on a false beard.

34. Bauer library. Midday

Long shot. TOMAS is ensconced in the deep windowsill above the couch, working: his feet against a typewriter, papers and notebooks in his lap. FRANCESCA kneels on the couch, looking up at him. She strokes his arm. TOMAS looks down, gently removes her arm.

TOMAS

You must leave.

FRANCESCA

It's all right. Arthur asked me to come and keep you company.

FRANCESCA gets up on the back of the couch so she is on the same level with TOMAS. She starts to undo his shirt. He pushes her hand away. She tries to embrace him. He is about to kiss her. A noise—from the hallway?

FRANCESCA pulls away, gets up.

> FRANCESCA

I must go now.

FRANCESCA leaves the room. TOMAS starts looking over the manuscripts again, making notations in his catalogue. Sighs. Thumbs through a few pages. He opens a notebook, skims a page in it, closes it again.

New shot. TOMAS goes to the desk. Picks up the phone, dials a number. He is calling INGRID.

> TOMAS

> (*On phone*) Listen, I have to stay here tonight. But can you meet me tomorrow afternoon? The Terrassen? Around four o'clock. . . . Okay. . . . Yes. . . . Sure, I'm all right. . . . So long.

He hangs up.

TOMAS turns to the small window above the desk, looks outside.

Long shot. BAUER enters. He is wearing a false beard. Stands on the far side of the desk.

> BAUER

Have there been any calls for me?

> TOMAS

No.

> BAUER

I've just received a very alarming message, delivered personally by one of my colleagues, that the police are after me, and that the phone is being tapped. There's only one way to deal with that problem, I'm afraid . . .

72

BAUER rips out the phone.

35. *Terrassen. Late afternoon, next day*

Camera tracks along tables of cafeteria until it reaches the table at which INGRID and TOMAS are seated opposite each other.

INGRID

I beg you. You must quit this job.

TOMAS

Give me—

INGRID

If you don't, it's over for us.

TOMAS

Give me a little more time.

TOMAS takes INGRID's hand. She pulls it away.

INGRID

I can't.

TOMAS

If I have to choose between them and you, of course I choose you.

INGRID

I don't believe you.

TOMAS

Give me five days more—till the weekend. I promise.

Medium close-up of INGRID.

I don't believe you.

36. *Ingrid's room. Night*

INGRID in close-up at a window. She is toying with something on the sill.

INGRID

I don't believe you . . . How can one believe anything as long as something else is going on at the same time? . . . It's never because of a reason someone gives that one person believes what another person says. Someone believing someone else only means that, once again, the strong are getting their way with people who don't know how to defend themselves.

37. *Bauer library. Day*

TOMAS alone, stacking up books. Goes out of frame, returns with more books. Goes out again. Returns holding BAUER's tape recorder. Sits down and turns it on.

TOMAS, in medium shot, listening to the tape recorder.

BAUER

(*Recorded*) I think the time is ripe for action. May I not be lacking in courage or in the necessary hardness of heart. Above all, no sentimentality.

BAUER's voice is covered over with the sounds of gunfire.

Close-up: TOMAS, his eyes closed. BAUER's tape recorder before him on the table.

TOMAS presses the "record" button, takes up the microphone. Stands up, carrying the machine. Paces back and forth as he speaks into it.

TOMAS

Tomas to Bauer. I hear you, Bauer. I hear everything you say. But it doesn't matter. I know how
to be stronger than you. You aren't going to kill
Francesca. You aren't dying yourself.

He sits down on the chair near the table. Presses button
to reverse the tape. Then presses "play" button.

TOMAS

(*Recorded*) But it doesn't matter. I know how
to be stronger than you. You aren't going to kill
Francesca. You aren't . . .

Sounds of gunfire (same as at the end of BAUER's voice)
cover the rest of the sentence.

TOMAS takes up the microphone again and presses "record"
button.

TOMAS

I know how to be stronger than you. One must
(1) have courage, (2) be patient, (3) be clear . . .

He pauses. Then continues speaking into the microphone.

TOMAS

All my understanding is *inside*.

Static on the tape, followed by BAUER's voice.

BAUER

(*Recorded*) And how is the work going?

TOMAS stares at the tape recorder. Then speaks, almost
tonelessly.

TOMAS

It's almost done. Another five days, I think.

The tape continues playing.

BAUER

(*Recorded*) Excellent. Then it's time for us to have a little talk about the future. You've become quite invaluable to me, Tomas. And not only is my wife fond of you but, despite our little differences from time to time, I've grown fond of you, too. I'm sure I can find more work for you to do here. In any case, I want you to stay on with us.

TOMAS

(*Coldly*) I'm afraid that's quite impossible. I have no desire to continue working for you.

TOMAS shuts off the tape recorder violently. Sound of door opening. TOMAS looks up.

Long shot of BAUER crossing the room (from TOMAS's point of view).

BAUER

My dear Tomas, how can you say that? Do you realize the importance of the work I do? Don't you realize—though it may be immodest of me to mention it—what an honor it is for you to assist me?

While talking, BAUER sits down opposite TOMAS. He takes a pack of cigarettes from a jacket pocket, holds it out to TOMAS.

BAUER

Cigarette?

TOMAS evidently refuses, for BAUER repockets the cigarettes
with a little smile.

BAUER

Don't you want to do something useful? Something
more than being a perpetual student, running
around to demonstrations or, like your girlfriend,
sitting in an office, peddling posters and pamphlets

exhorting people to support noble aims they have no idea how to carry out? I'm giving you a chance to *do* something, by helping me.

Two-shot, from behind BAUER.

TOMAS

It's out of the question.

BAUER

And the confidence I've placed in you? Doesn't that count for anything? I assure you it's not just anyone whom I would trust as I have you.

TOMAS raises BAUER's tape recorder so he can see it.

TOMAS

Dr. Bauer, let me assure you that your trust is entirely misplaced. You have no reason to trust me.

BAUER

But I do, Tomas, I do. Whatever you say or show me, I shall continue to trust you. I understand human nature, my dear Tomas. I might add, it is very useful for my work. Believe me, I'm never wrong in my judgment of people.

TOMAS

Well, you are wrong about me. If you don't believe that, I'll make you believe it.

TOMAS jumps up.

BAUER

Are you threatening me with violence?

Camera follows TOMAS, going toward the desk. He reaches in back of the books on a shelf next to the desk for the revolver.

Long shot of the two. BAUER stands near the desk now, holding an identical revolver in his hand, pointing it at TOMAS.

> BAUER
>
> Are you looking for one like this?

> TOMAS
>
> Where did you get that?

> BAUER
>
> From the same person who gave you yours. She worries about both of us, Tomas. She wants us both to be safe.

TOMAS takes his hand off his revolver, sits down heavily.

> BAUER
>
> Good. Then I can put mine away.

BAUER puts the revolver back in his pocket.

> BAUER
>
> Now we can talk reasonably. I just want you to reconsider your decision about staying with us. Don't make up your mind now. That's all I ask.

38. *A city bridge. Day*

Very long shot: TOMAS walking across the bridge.

TOMAS'S VOICE

"Bauer had given me the following Sunday off. I sent a note to Ingrid, suggesting we go out in the boat."

39. *Outdoors (water, shore). Day*

Long shot: TOMAS and INGRID in a motorboat, TOMAS at the wheel. She in slacks and a bulky sweater; he in jeans, a sweater, boots, a heavy coat. They seem happy together. Suddenly the boat swerves sharply.

TOMAS

I have to pull in.

INGRID

Tomas!

Two-shot of BAUER and FRANCESCA, arm in arm, standing on the shore. BAUER has a bandage on his head, binoculars hanging from his neck.

Back to the boat, which has pulled ashore. INGRID grabs TOMAS as he starts to get out. He pulls away from her, jumps off the boat, and joins the BAUERS. TOMAS looks at FRANCESCA. BAUER hands TOMAS a hat like his, and sunglasses.

Camera pans to follow the three as they walk away and disappear into the woods. Dvořák through entire sequence.

40. *Hallway and bedroom of Bauer house. Night*

The hallway. Medium shot: TOMAS, alone. He is listening by the bedroom door. We hear BAUER shouting, but the words can't be distinguished.

> TOMAS'S VOICE
> "They were quarreling again."

> BAUER
> (*Off*) If you say another word, I'll kill you!

Silence.

Another shot of TOMAS.

> TOMAS'S VOICE
> "But she hadn't said a word."

Noise of slaps, FRANCESCA's cries, something breaking. TOMAS bursts into the room.

In the bedroom. A two-shot: FRANCESCA in a nightgown is sitting in a chair, winding yarn into a ball. In another chair, opposite her, BAUER, wearing striped pajamas, sits with his arms outstretched, holding the yarn for her to wind. BAUER looks up.

> BAUER
> (*To* TOMAS) What are you doing up at this hour? Is anything wrong? Aren't you feeling well?

FRANCESCA looks concerned. She drops the ball of yarn, which rolls across the floor (camera follows it)—BAUER comes into frame from the left, on his knees. He begins to wind it up.

Cut to FRANCESCA and TOMAS embracing.

Cut to BAUER, still kneeling on the floor.

> BAUER
>
> I think you've alarmed my wife. You see how much she cares about you.

New shot. FRANCESCA looks down at BAUER. Walks over, motions for him to stand up, then to get into the closet or armoire. She locks BAUER in. BAUER resists a little. Then she returns to TOMAS. They kiss, then lie down together on the large bed and begin to make love.

41. *Bauer bedroom. Same night, later*

Sequence opens with a shot of TOMAS and FRANCESCA sleeping in the bed. TOMAS has his arm over FRANCESCA. The sound of rhythmical knocking coming from the closet (same rhythm and approximately same volume as hammering sound heard at the opening of the film). TOMAS wakes up, sits up. FRANCESCA is still asleep. He shakes her.

>   TOMAS
> (*Whispering*) We can't leave him in there all night.

FRANCESCA turns over. TOMAS shakes her again.

>   FRANCESCA
> (*Sleepily*) It's all right. You don't understand. Go to sleep.

TOMAS leans over her.

>   TOMAS
> (*Louder*) Unlock the door! If you don't, I will.

>   FRANCESCA
> It isn't necessary. He has his own key.

More knocking.

TOMAS in closer shot from the side of the bed. He has thrown the covers off himself.

>   TOMAS
> I don't believe you.

(*Off*) Then ask him yourself.

More knocking from inside the closet. TOMAS gets out of bed.

New shot: TOMAS stands in front of the closet. He knocks back twice. The inside knocking stops.

Close-up of the back of TOMAS's head.

TOMAS

Bauer! If you can, come out! Now!

Medium shot taken from behind TOMAS. The door opens. BAUER steps out fully dressed (suit, hat, unbuttoned coat, spectacles). TOMAS steps back, out of frame. BAUER turns to FRANCESCA in bed.

BAUER

I must go out, darling.

FRANCESCA

At this hour? It's so cold. Can't it wait until morning?

BAUER

(*To* FRANCESCA) I'm afraid not. You know— (*To* TOMAS) —how emergencies come up in political work. Those of us who devote ourselves to obscure embattled causes must be willing to sacrifice mere personal convenience from time to time.

BAUER has crossed the room. He turns to FRANCESCA, blows her a kiss. Starts toward the door again, then takes two steps backward, as if he'd forgotten something. He shakes hands with TOMAS. Leaves.

Shot of bedroom door closing slowly.

42. Ingrid's room. Still later that night

Medium-long shot. INGRID is sitting on the edge of the
bed, wearing a white terrycloth bathrobe, looking very
uncomfortable, evidently on her guard.

BAUER

(*Off*) It's very kind of you to see me at such a late
hour.

INGRID

I've been trying to see you—at least talk to you—
for weeks. You kept refusing, and then suddenly
you turn up here without even phoning first.

Another medium-long shot: BAUER (from INGRID's point
of view) sitting in the comfortable chair. BAUER, dressed
as in the previous sequence (minus overcoat and scarf)
and smoking a pipe, is at his most charming. He shakes
his head self-deprecatingly.

BAUER

It isn't that I didn't *want* to see you. But the
way it is in my house, I couldn't find the op-
portunity until now.

He pauses, leans forward.

BAUER

You see, I'm watched.

Medium-long shot of INGRID.

INGRID

By your wife? Hasn't she something else to occupy
her mind these days?

Back to BAUER, who looks hurt.

BAUER

Would you mind if I took off my jacket? I'm
a little warm.

BAUER stands. Goes over to table. He removes his jacket,
folds it, and lays it carefully over a chair. He wipes
his brow. Suddenly he seems about to faint. Alarmed,
INGRID gets up and comes over to him.

90

INGRID

Shall I open a window?

BAUER

No, I'm all right. For a moment I was feeling
faint, but it's passed now.

He sits down.

INGRID

(*Hesitatingly*) But aren't you—ill?

After a moment's hesitation, she also sits.

Two-shot of BAUER and INGRID facing each other across
the table. BAUER smiles affably.

BAUER

Good God, no! I couldn't be healthier, knock on
wood. . . . Did Tomas tell you that? It must be
one of Francesca's stories. I shudder to think of the
tales she's been feeding him.

BAUER's affability has turned to melancholy. He shakes
his head. Despite her prejudices against him, INGRID has
visibly started to relax. BAUER is much more pleasant
and reasonable than she'd expected—and more appealing
as a man. There is a slight undercurrent of flirtatiousness
in everything she says in the rest of the sequence.

INGRID

You know why I wanted to see you? Because
I consider you my enemy.

BAUER puffs on his pipe, looking benevolent and understanding.

BAUER

Why?

INGRID

Because of what's happened to Tomas since he
began working for you.

BAUER

(*Wistfully*) You think I have some influence over
him?

INGRID

More than that. I don't know what to call it . . .
But I warn you, I intend to fight for him.

INGRID's old suspicions have returned. BAUER smiles.

BAUER

My dear Ingrid, I wish it were true. But I'm
afraid I have no influence over him whatever.

INGRID

And your wife?

BAUER seems to hesitate.

INGRID

Tell me the truth.

BAUER

That's another story, I'm afraid. A very old one,
too, isn't it? An aging man with a beautiful wife
has to expect these situations, I suppose, and meet
them with resignation . . .

INGRID looks as if she is about to cry.

BAUER

But I'm speaking too bluntly. Forgive me. I know
you must be thinking of Tomas.

INGRID forces back her tears. She looks at BAUER appraisingly, taking in even more fully the fact that he is a good-looking man.

INGRID

Yes, I was. But I was also looking at you.

BAUER reaches over for INGRID's hand. She almost takes it away, then changes her mind. (Wagner phrase.) They stare at each other for a moment. Then INGRID does pull away her hand and stand up. She moves a little behind BAUER's chair. He tilts his head back to look at her for a moment, then leans forward again.

INGRID

But your wife and Tomas . . .

BAUER shakes his head.

BAUER

At the moment, I fear, I can do nothing about it . . .

He looks up again at INGRID.

BAUER

Perhaps if you and I joined forces . . .

INGRID has come back to the table and sits down slowly.

INGRID

To do what?

43. *Bauer dining room. The next evening*

The sequence opens with a long shot: INGRID, TOMAS, FRANCESCA, and BAUER at dinner. BAUER's table manners are, for him, restrained. He has on his dark glasses

and wears a quilted or silk lounging jacket and a foulard.
The table has a festive appearance: flowers and several
bottles of wine, etc.

INGRID'S VOICE

"Bauer was reminiscing about his political
career . . ."

Closer shot of the four.

BAUER

Perhaps I was more idealistic in those days . . .

INGRID

You mean more revolutionary?

BAUER smiles patronizingly.

BAUER

The revolution isn't coming soon.

INGRID

When is the time for revolution?

BAUER

Either too early or too late.

INGRID

Then that's the right time.

More eating. Suddenly BAUER stops eating and pushes
his plate away.

BAUER

There's something wrong with the food!

He coughs violently. INGRID looks alarmed.

TOMAS

(Off) What's the matter? It tastes all right to me.

BAUER bangs on the table. MRS. GRUNDBERG comes in.

> BAUER
>
> Take this away! And you can pack your things!
> We won't need you any more!

MRS. GRUNDBERG clears the table and goes out.

> BAUER
>
> (*Whispering*) I think the food is poisoned!

INGRID looks even more alarmed at the scene with MRS.
GRUNDBERG: this is the side of BAUER she hasn't seen.
FRANCESCA reaches for her hand across the table to re-
assure her.

> TOMAS
>
> Ingrid?

INGRID looks at him irritably.

> INGRID
>
> What?

> TOMAS
>
> Nothing.

BAUER seems in an exceptionally good mood now. He
fills everyone's wineglass again. INGRID finishes her glass.
BAUER starts to refill it.

> TOMAS
>
> Don't drink any more. You know it makes you
> sick.

INGRID ignores TOMAS, turns to BAUER.

> INGRID
>
> Thanks.

Group shot: INGRID, FRANCESCA, and BAUER. FRANCESCA looks at INGRID.

FRANCESCA

I propose a toast to our guest.

BAUER

Excellent idea. To the lovely Ingrid.

Medium shot of TOMAS: he empties his glass quickly, holds it out to BAUER (who is out of frame) to be refilled. The camera moves back to include BAUER in the shot. TOMAS still holding out his glass. BAUER shakes his head, smiling.

BAUER

I think you've had enough, my boy. I want you to have a clear head for tomorrow's work.

TOMAS is about to object, when BAUER claps his hands sharply and pushes back his chair. His movements and voice are hearty, ostentatiously host-like.

BAUER

Shall we go into the living room?

Everyone gets up, except TOMAS.

BAUER

Oh, Tomas, I want you to do something for me.

TOMAS stands, hurls his napkin down on the table. BAUER puts his arm on TOMAS's shoulder, whispers something to him.

Long shot of the two women standing together, talking, in the living room.

Back to TOMAS and BAUER. TOMAS looks sullen. We don't

hear what BAUER is saying, but we see BAUER extract some money from his wallet and give it to TOMAS. (It is a month's advance wages for MRS. GRUNDBERG.) At the end BAUER's voice becomes audible. His tone is venomous.

BAUER

And then drive her into town. I don't want that old woman in this house a minute longer than necessary!

BAUER goes toward the living room. TOMAS, left alone in the shot, goes through the door to the kitchen.

44. Bauer living room. An hour later

The room is darkened. Camera pans slowly over long wall of living room, past the large landscape painting, past a pornographic film being projected on the wall, arriving at the couch where BAUER and INGRID are making love (INGRID is straddling BAUER's lap). They are partly dressed. Their movements are convulsive, without tenderness. Sound of a movie projector running.

Medium close-up of the movie projector and its smoky beam of light.

Medium close-up of FRANCESCA in a chair. She is watching something intently.

After a moment, one hand comes up to partly cover her mouth.

BAUER is lying on top of INGRID on the couch.

Back to FRANCESCA, who looks up.

Medium-long shot that includes FRANCESCA and the two making love and TOMAS, who has apparently just returned and stands watching on the far side of the room. He has on his leather jacket and holds the car keys.

TOMAS
(*Softly*) Francesca?

FRANCESCA puts her fingers to her lips.

FRANCESCA
Shhhhh . . .

INGRID cries out with pleasure. FRANCESCA signals TOMAS not to speak.

Back to TOMAS. He zips up his jacket and seems about to leave.

FRANCESCA
Come here.

TOMAS approaches the chair. FRANCESCA motions for him to sit at her feet, his back against her legs and his head leaning back on her knees.

Two-shot (from the far side of the couch): FRANCESCA and TOMAS sitting on the floor. She puts one hand on his forehead, turns his head toward the couch.

45. *Bauer library. Next morning*

TOMAS is working, standing up, with great energy. The room is a mess.

BAUER enters, carrying a cup of coffee. His manner is casual, friendly. He's wearing his pajamas and a dressing gown.

> BAUER
>
> Good morning. Did you sleep well?

TOMAS turns. Glares at him without answering.

> BAUER
>
> About our conversation last week. I want to know what you've decided.

Change of shot. Still no answer from TOMAS, who goes on working.

> BAUER
>
> You will stay on, won't you? I mean, after the work is done.

BAUER comes over to TOMAS.

> BAUER
>
> Don't you want to stay? Look at me . . . Tell me the truth.

TOMAS goes to the blackboard. Writes on it:

> What could make me want to stay?

BAUER stands behind him, takes the chalk from his hand. He writes, underneath:
> A gun.
> A woman.
> A cause.
> The wish to destroy me.
> The wish to destroy yourself.

TOMAS turns, and looks at BAUER again.

TOMAS

Where is Ingrid?

BAUER

That's right. Talk to her first.

46. Bauer dining room. Shortly after

INGRID is arranging a breakfast tray: eggs, toast, coffee,
a flower in a slender Japanese vase. Perhaps she is wearing
MRS. GRUNDBERG's apron. TOMAS grabs her roughly around
the shoulder from behind. She hadn't seen him.

TOMAS

What the hell are you doing?

INGRID

Don't!

TOMAS

Who is that for?

INGRID

Francesca woke up with a headache.

TOMAS is furious and barely able to control his anger,
most of which is toward BAUER but which he is taking
out on INGRID.

TOMAS

You're damned right she has a headache. So do
I. And so should you—

He starts pulling her away from the tray. Now INGRID
is angry.

100

INGRID

Stop it! Since when do you tell me how to be-
have? If you want to talk, you'll have to wait
until I've brought this upstairs. . . . Or can't you
bear that I've taken the same freedom as you?

TOMAS slaps her hard across the face. She barely flinches.

INGRID

Is that what you wanted to say?

TOMAS looks at her, confused and remorseful and still
angry.

TOMAS

Listen, this morning Bauer had the nerve to ask
me to stay, to go on working for him . . . And . . .
and there's something in me that wants to say
yes. . . . That's what I wanted to tell you. Not
about last night. . . . Let's take a walk. Help me
to think. I don't think I can get out of here unless
you remind me why I have to. Tell me all the
reasons for saying no.

Medium close-up of INGRID.

INGRID

But I don't see why you should go. It's valuable
work, the Bauers treat you as one of the family,
the pay is good. Why *don't* you stay? If the
reason is me—all those objections I used to raise
to your being away too much—there's no problem.

TOMAS stares at her, hardly believing his ears. He speaks
very slowly, trying to remain calm.

TOMAS

What do you mean?

Francesca asked me this morning to stay on. Help her run the household. Take care of her correspondence. Accompany her on trips—she goes back and forth to Italy all the time. . . . It would be only a part-time job . . .

TOMAS tries to control his rising hysteria.

TOMAS

And you said—?

INGRID

Not a definite yes. I said I'd have to discuss it with you first.

TOMAS

Which is what we're doing now. Right?

INGRID nods.

TOMAS

You're telling me you want to stay. Right? Here! With the Bauers! . . . Are you saying that?

INGRID

Not exactly. . . . Yes, I am willing to stay on— if you are.

TOMAS

That's your answer? And your advice to me, too?

INGRID

Well, you haven't taken much advice from me yet. Whatever I say, you'll do what *you* want, won't you?

TOMAS grabs INGRID by the shoulders and shouts hoarsely.

TOMAS

Now listen to me! I'm going to do one of three things. I'll beat the hell out of you. I'll walk out of here with you. Or I'll leave here alone. . . . You can choose. Which is it to be?

INGRID

Francesca's breakfast is getting cold.

TOMAS

If you pick up that tray and put just one foot on those stairs—

FRANCESCA

(*Off*) Ingrid! I'm hungry.

INGRID picks up the tray.

INGRID

Wait!

FRANCESCA

(*Off*) Ingrid!

INGRID looks despairingly at TOMAS, picks up the tray, and rushes up the stairs. TOMAS goes toward the front door.

47. A marina. Midday

Medium-long shot: TOMAS sleeping in an uncomfortable position on the floor of the motorboat, inside a sleeping bag. He has several days' growth of beard. Boat rocking with the motion of the water. Sounds of birds' cries, of water slapping against the sides of the boats.

"I couldn't go back to Ingrid's place. I felt absolutely numb, and tired enough to sleep for a year—"

48. The motorboat. Afternoon, several days later

Very long shot: TOMAS has moved the boat a hundred yards from the marina and dropped anchor there. He is sitting in the rear of the boat, a blanket over his shoulders. His voice continues from the previous scene.

TOMAS'S VOICE
"—but I only slept the first two days."

49. *Bauer dining room. Evening*

Close-up of INGRID's face. She looks calm and somehow older. Her eyes seem slightly unfocused.

After holding the shot for several seconds, the camera moves back to show INGRID serving dinner to the BAUERS. (She is already firmly installed in the BAUER establishment—as an amateur servant, inheriting some tasks of the housekeeper who was fired, and as companion to FRANCESCA.) There are only two chairs at one end of the table, which the BAUERS occupy.

Medium shot of the BAUERS at the table. FRANCESCA has just taken a slice of roast and begun cutting it. Now BAUER is helping himself to four slices. INGRID comes next to him and holds out the dish of boiled potatoes. As BAUER takes some, he smiles at INGRID. This seems to displease FRANCESCA.

> FRANCESCA
> Not enough salt, I'm sorry to say, Ingrid dear.

> BAUER
> Now, darling, you must be patient with Ingrid. Considering her inexperience, she's done remarkably well. . . . Think how lucky we are that she's helping us out in this unhappy emergency.

Two-shot of INGRID and FRANCESCA.

> FRANCESCA
> Ingrid knows how grateful we are. Don't you?

FRANCESCA reaches out and strokes INGRID's hand. INGRID

105

flinches slightly—her breathing is shorter—then she seems to accept the caress and be comforted by it.

> FRANCESCA
> Did you eat, cara? You look pale.

INGRID shakes her head.

> FRANCESCA
> Why then, you must sit with us. Isn't that right, Arthur? . . . I had no idea you were hungry.

Medium-long shot. BAUER gets up, goes out of shot, and returns with another chair, which he places at the corner of the table, between himself and FRANCESCA. They are close on either side of her.

Medium shot. FRANCESCA takes a forkful of food and puts it in INGRID's mouth, giggling a little. INGRID starts to chew solemnly, but FRANCESCA's gaiety is contagious. She begins to giggle, too. BAUER has an expression of mock-annoyance.

> BAUER
> What is this levity at my table? I won't have it!

FRANCESCA puts another forkful into INGRID's mouth. The two women begin to laugh unrestrainedly. BAUER looks at them quizzically, then takes up his fork, spears a piece of meat with it, and puts it near INGRID's lips. She snaps off the piece of meat like a playful young animal. BAUER laughs. Now all three are laughing and feeding each other food. Food is dribbling down BAUER's chin. The laughter becomes increasingly wild, as the camera tracks in.

50. Bauer bedroom. Night

FRANCESCA seated in the alcove at the table, putting on eye shadow and false eyelashes. INGRID watches, with an almost trance-like look, like a small child watching its mother.

FRANCESCA turns to INGRID, smiles. Motions for INGRID to sit next to her.

FRANCESCA

Come.

Closer shot of the two sitting side by side on the bench in front of the dressing table. FRANCESCA puts some eye make-up on INGRID. INGRID sits passively, then leans forward to look more closely at herself in the mirror.

FRANCESCA

Do you like it?

INGRID

Yes.

FRANCESCA turns more fully toward INGRID and smiles fondly.

FRANCESCA

I'm going to speak Italian with you.

INGRID

Sure.

FRANCESCA touches INGRID's hair playfully.

FRANCESCA

Capelli.

INGRID repeats shyly.

INGRID

Capelli.

FRANCESCA touches her own eyes.

FRANCESCA

Occhi.

INGRID

Occhi.

FRANCESCA looks at INGRID appraisingly.

> FRANCESCA
>
> Hai un bel naso.

INGRID touches her own nose with embarrassment.

> INGRID
>
> Naso.

FRANCESCA strokes her own lips.

> FRANCESCA
>
> Bocca.

> INGRID
>
> Bocca.

INGRID puts one hand on her breast.

> INGRID
>
> What's the word for this?

FRANCESCA smiles with amusement.

> FRANCESCA
>
> Corpo.

FRANCESCA makes a melodramatic gesture, crossing both hands on her own breast.

> FRANCESCA
>
> E anima.

INGRID repeats softly.

> INGRID
>
> Corpo e anima.

FRANCESCA turns away and looks at INGRID in the mirror.

FRANCESCA

Ce l'hai una parrucca?

INGRID

No.

FRANCESCA

Vuoi provare la mia?

INGRID

Yes.

FRANCESCA lifts up the top of the dressing table, takes out a blond wig, and fits it on INGRID's head.

FRANCESCA

Ti piace?

INGRID

(*Laughing*) No.

FRANCESCA

Neanche a me.

FRANCESCA takes off the blond wig, brings out a black wig.

FRANCESCA

Prova questa qui.

INGRID puts the wig on herself, studies herself in the mirror.

INGRID

Now I look like you.

FRANCESCA

Questa va meglio.

FRANCESCA looks at INGRID for a moment, then gets up.

110

FRANCESCA

Aspetta. Ho una cosa per te.

Wagner phrase starts. FRANCESCA goes out of frame, leaving INGRID staring at herself in the mirror. When FRANCESCA comes back into the shot, the music fades. FRANCESCA is carrying a pair of evening pajamas. She holds them out to INGRID. INGRID stands up, takes them, starts to undress in order to try them on (her back is to the camera). FRANCESCA sits on the bench watching her. INGRID puts on the pants, then the top, which she is unable to fasten.

INGRID

There's no button.

FRANCESCA takes a safety pin from the dressing table and closes the blouse, all the time staring up into INGRID's face. INGRID seems completely passive now. FRANCESCA stands, takes INGRID by the arm, and sits her down again in front of the dressing table. FRANCESCA stands behind INGRID, her hands on INGRID's shoulders, her body against INGRID's back. INGRID turns her head and looks up at FRANCESCA questioningly.

51. Bauer bedroom. Night

Long shot of the large double bed. BAUER and FRANCESCA are propped up on pillows; both are wearing glasses and look quite unglamorous. FRANCESCA is reading *Amica;* BAUER is reading a heavy dark book whose title we don't see. INGRID, between them, lies farther down in the bed; her arms are crossed. She is wearing more

111

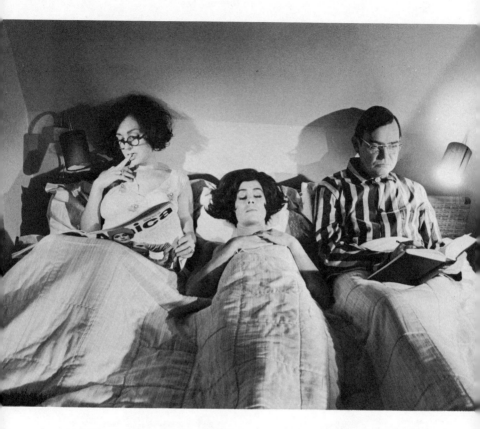

make-up than usual and has on the black wig. BAUER
yawns, puts down the book, and switches off the lamp
on his side of the bed.

BAUER

Do you have enough light, darling?

FRANCESCA

One moment.

Close-up: INGRID looks shyly at each of them in turn.

Medium shot (slowly traveling back): FRANCESCA puts the magazine on the floor and turns off her lamp. The room is still faintly lit. At the same moment they turn toward INGRID and descend on her, covering her completely from view.

52. Stairs, hallway in Bauer house. Morning

Long shot: BAUER in dressing gown and leather slippers comes from the front hallway to the foot of the stairs carrying several pieces of mail. He flips through the letters and immediately rips one open. Reads it, smiles, leans against the banister, with an air of triumph.

> TOMAS'S VOICE
>
> "Dr. Bauer, are you open to proposals of ransom— or at least an exchange of hostages? If so, I've an offer to make: my return to your household if you'll let Ingrid go. I'm sure I can be of more use to you than she can. The deal depends on her remaining ignorant of our arrangement."

BAUER folds the letter and puts it in the pocket of his dressing gown. He mounts the stairs rapidly. The camera holds on the empty stairs. The silence is broken by INGRID's voice coming from upstairs. She is crying.

> INGRID
>
> (Off) No, please don't send me away! What did I do?

53. *Marina. Ten days later*

TOMAS is tying the motorboat to the dock. He looks unwashed, haggard, and even more unshaven.

> TOMAS'S VOICE
>
> "I had proposed a bargain which the Bauers accepted. They had fulfilled their part of it, but still I delayed going through with mine."

Long shot: a man is pedaling down the dock on a bicycle. When he gets close, he tosses an envelope into TOMAS's boat, makes a turn without stopping, and rides off out of sight.

> TOMAS
>
> Hey!

TOMAS reaches down, picks up the envelope, opens it, takes out a letter. He reads it, frowning.

> TOMAS'S VOICE
>
> "From Bauer. Telling me that I am impatiently expected."

54. *Ingrid's room. Late afternoon*

Close-up of a bearded young man's face. The camera moves back: he is standing on his head (yoga style) against a wall, naked except for BVD's. It's LARS, INGRID's new lover.

Cut to TOMAS at the door.

Where is Ingrid?

Back to LARS, who motions toward the window with one foot, almost losing his balance. INGRID comes through the window from the roof, jumps down, closes the window. She looks at TOMAS impassively.

INGRID
What are you doing here?

Medium-long shot: INGRID and TOMAS face each other (we see them in profile). LARS is between them and to the rear, feet up; we can't see his head.

TOMAS
You've changed your hair.

INGRID
You're going back, aren't you?

TOMAS nods.

INGRID
And you can't tell me why!

TOMAS shakes his head. He goes to the bed, pulls out a cheap suitcase from underneath; goes once out of frame (to a chest of drawers) and returns with some shirts and underwear, throws them in the suitcase. Then he goes to the closet (between the sink and the wall where the BAUER poster used to be; it's been taken down) and takes out more clothes. While at the closet, he looks over his shoulder, making an impatient gesture with his head in LARS's direction.

TOMAS
Who's he?

115

INGRID

Aren't you taking your books?

TOMAS returns with some pants to the bed, throws them in the suitcase. INGRID stands behind him.

INGRID

I loved you, you know.

TOMAS trying to close the suitcase; one snap-lock doesn't close. He answers her without looking up.

TOMAS

You don't any more?

INGRID

No.

TOMAS picks up suitcase, moves toward door. Camera follows him.

Loud noise, like someone jumping. LARS has gotten back on his feet.

Medium-long shot: TOMAS by the door. LARS standing possessively by INGRID.

TOMAS

But I love you. I'm sure I do.

INGRID

Get out!

LARS puts his arm around INGRID. The door slams.

55. *The street. Two hours later*

Long shot: TOMAS sits on top of a low wall on the

corner of the street in front of INGRID's apartment building, suitcase at his feet. He is smoking.

Low-angle shot of the façade of INGRID's building.

Another long shot of TOMAS looking up. He throws away his cigarette.

Closer shot: TOMAS stands up, leans against a tree.

56. *Entrance to Bauer house. Next day*

Medium shot: TOMAS knocking on the door. BAUER opens cautiously. He is wearing a tuxedo. Almost immediately, BAUER tries to shut the door. TOMAS prevents him.

> TOMAS
> What's wrong?

BAUER stops trying to close the door and TOMAS takes a step back. Both men are breathing heavily.

> BAUER
> I'm afraid I can't let you in. . . . As you know, while I'm capable of overlooking many things—

> TOMAS
> What the hell are you talking about?

> BAUER
> —Francesca isn't as tolerant as I am.

TOMAS starts pushing again, but BAUER still manages to block the door.

117

BAUER

I'm sorry, Tomas, but my wife doesn't want to see you any more.

Again, TOMAS attempts to force his way past BAUER.

TOMAS

(*Shouting*) I don't believe you! . . . Let me talk to her!

BAUER

I can't. She refuses to see you. Besides, she's very ill.

Change of shot (camera is inside house, behind BAUER). TOMAS is still struggling.

TOMAS

You're lying! You're hiding something from me!

BAUER's look changes from self-righteous coldness to fear.

BAUER

Stop!

TOMAS

You've killed her!

TOMAS breaks past BAUER.

57. Inside Bauer house: stairs, bedroom. Same day

Long shot from the top of the stairs: TOMAS runs up. He pauses before the bedroom door. We hear the sound of hammering from beyond the door. He flings open the door.

Long shot: a CARPENTER is nailing the last boards in a simple pine coffin. The room is filled with flowers; the curtains are drawn. FRANCESCA, wearing a long white dress, lies on the bed in the classic corpse position, arms crossed. The lamps on both sides of the bed have been replaced by candles, and flowers put on the night-tables.

Shot (from inside room) of TOMAS standing in the door-way.

Closer shot: the CARPENTER finishes the coffin, replaces the hammer in a tool chest, stands. BAUER, breathless, arrives at the open door.

> CARPENTER
> Do you need me to help you?

> BAUER
> No. That will be all.

The CARPENTER leaves. Footsteps going down the stairs.

Change of shot: TOMAS sitting on the edge of the bed. He brushes FRANCESCA's lips with his fingertips.

Medium close-up (from side of bed) of FRANCESCA's face.

Back to three-shot. BAUER stands above TOMAS.

> BAUER
> I know you don't understand, but you must believe one thing—that I loved her. I loved her with all my heart.

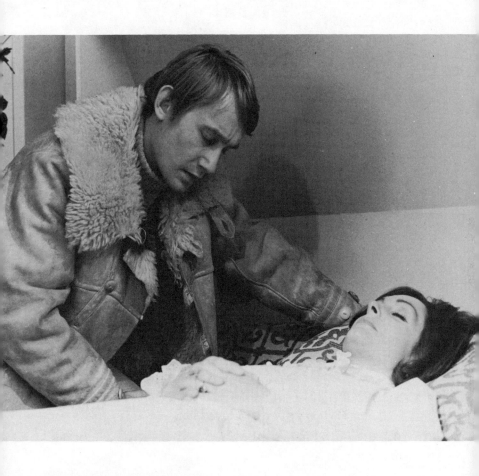

TOMAS looks up.

TOMAS

And that's why you killed her?

BAUER

I didn't! If you must know . . . she killed herself. She's been ill too long. She couldn't bear that any more.

TOMAS

You killed her. Why don't you tell the truth?

BAUER

Let me show you the suicide note.

BAUER fumbles in his pocket.

TOMAS

What does that prove? You could have written it yourself. Or made her write it.

BAUER lets his hand fall.

BAUER

You really think I had so much power over her?

TOMAS

Didn't you?

BAUER laughs, but then it turns into a kind of gasping and dry sobbing. He falls across FRANCESCA's legs and buries his face in his hands.

BAUER

All right, I killed her. . . . Still, you *must* believe me when I say that I loved her.

He sits up, clutches at TOMAS's sleeve. TOMAS pulls his arm away.

TOMAS

Nothing you can say or do could make me believe that.

BAUER

Nothing?

BAUER pulls out the small revolver and points it at his chest.

TOMAS

Don't do that!

BAUER fires, collapses at the foot of the bed. TOMAS jumps up, heads for the door. Camera follows him.

FRANCESCA

(*Off*) Tomas!

TOMAS wheels around.

Cut to bed. FRANCESCA is sitting up. TOMAS slowly crosses the room. Holds out his hand. She takes it; then turns away from him and crouches over BAUER's body. She opens his jacket, puts her ear on his chest. Sighs.

FRANCESCA
He wanted so much to die. But he didn't know how.

TOMAS sits on the edge of the coffin. FRANCESCA takes the gun and hands it to TOMAS. Still on the bed, she moves away from BAUER's body and looks calmly at TOMAS.

TOMAS
Is it really so hard to die? So complicated?

FRANCESCA
Yes, it is . . . Unless it's very easy.

Closer shot of TOMAS. He looks at her quizzically.

TOMAS
But you were helping him.

He looks as if he has just understood something. He points the gun at his chest.

FRANCESCA
(Off) Wait.

58. Yard of Bauer house. Late afternoon

Very long shot (taken from second-floor window of the house): TOMAS and FRANCESCA have made a bonfire and are burning BAUER's manuscripts and papers. They

124

play like children, laughing and breaking off several times to embrace each other.

Medium close-up of the fire.

Entire sequence covered by Dvořák quartet.

59. *Exterior of Bauer house. Early morning*

Very long shot of the house, from beyond the surrounding wall. It seems completely quiet, closed up.

60. *Entrance of Bauer house. Afternoon*

Long shot: INGRID knocks impatiently on the door (same rhythm as hammering noise). FRANCESCA opens it, stares at her coldly.

INGRID

Where is he?

FRANCESCA stands aside, without saying a word.

61. *Interior of Bauer house: living room, dining room, kitchen, library. A minute later*

Long shot: TOMAS sitting at the desk. His head is bandaged. He is playing one of BAUER's tapes; it is full of static.

BAUER

(*Recorded*) I think the time is ripe for action. May I not be lacking in courage or in the necessary hardness of heart. Above all, no sentimentality.

Camera tracks in close.

Long shot of FRANCESCA in doorway (from TOMAS's view).

New shot (from doorway: FRANCESCA's view): INGRID leans over TOMAS at the desk, holding his head. He doesn't respond. She kneels down, begins to weep.

INGRID

Forgive me, forgive me, forgive me.

INGRID begins unwinding bandage. TOMAS neither assists nor prevents her.

New shot of FRANCESCA, standing in the center of the room, watching them. Back to TOMAS and INGRID, who, still kneeling before TOMAS, has begun to wind end of bandage around her own head. FRANCESCA comes into the shot, stands behind them, watching impassively. TOMAS looks up at her. FRANCESCA puts her arm lightly on TOMAS's shoulder. He looks at INGRID.

TOMAS

Let's go.

FRANCESCA takes her hand away.

62. *Street to the side of Bauer house. Later*

Long shot: INGRID and TOMAS hurry through the side gate, almost at a run. A Volkswagen is parked just outside. INGRID gets in the driver's seat, which is nearer to the camera; TOMAS on the other side. Dvořák from start of sequence to the end.

Low-angle long shot (taken from street) of living-room window. BAUER and FRANCESCA are looking down calmly. This tableau behind the window has the calm and benign stiffness of an old-fashioned wedding portrait. Sounds: the slamming of a car door and the car motor starting up.

Long shot: the car drives from right to left out of the frame.

63. Road. *Still later*

Very long shot of the Volkswagen (from behind) speeding down a country road, receding into the distance. Dvořák.

64. Sea. *Day*

Very long shot of frozen sea. Dvořák. White fade.